Romulus and Remus

The Twins Who Made Rome
Ancient Roman Mythology
Children's Greek & Roman Books

BABY PROFESSOR

EDUCATION KIDS

Speedy Publishing LLC

40 E. Main St. #1156

Newark, DE 19711

www.speedypublishing.com

Copyright 2017

In this book, we're going to cover the legend of Romulus and Remus, the founders of Rome. So, let's get right to it!

WHO WERE ROMULUS AND REMUS?

The story of the twins Romulus and Remus is most likely a mixture of truth and myth. To understand their story, you need to know a little about the history of the events in Ancient Greece and Ancient Rome that took place before they were born.

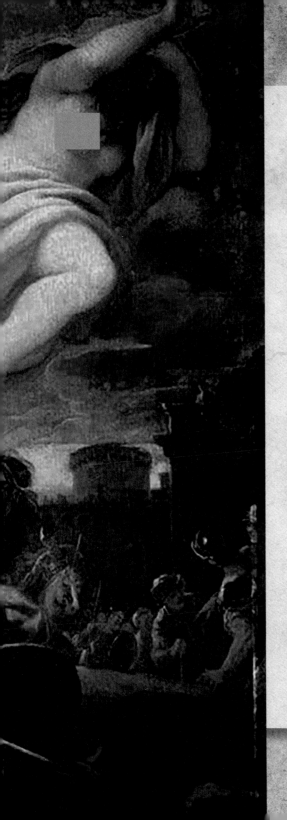

Romulus and Remus were descended from Aeneas. Aeneas was a Trojan hero in Greek mythology. He's described In Homer's famous poem, The Iliad.

His exciting adventures to discover the lands of Italy were written about by another famous author called Virgil. The Aeneid by Virgil is an epic poem that tells about the history and founding of the city of Rome.

The twins were related to Aeneas by their mother's father, their grandfather, who was named Numitor. Numitor was the king of a city called Alba Longa. This ancient city was part of Latium in the middle of the lands we now know as Italy. Before the twins were born, Numitor's younger brother who was named Amulius decided he wanted to be king.

AMULIUS GAINS CONTROL OF ALBA LONGA

In order to get control over the kingdom, Amulius gained control over the treasury and riches of the city. Once he did that, he was able to take over the kingdom. But it wasn't enough that he had banished Numitor. Amulius wanted to make sure Numitor's sons wouldn't take over, so he killed them. Numitor had a daughter as well and her name was Rhea Silvia.

Amulius made sure that Rhea Silvia wouldn't have any children who could fight him for the throne of Alba Longa in the future. He forced her to be a Vestal Virgin. Vestal Virgins were sacred priestesses of the goddess, Vesta. Their role was to keep fires burning in the hearth of homes. They took vows of chastity, which meant that they never married or had children.

WHO WAS THE FATHER OF ROMULUS AND REMUS?

There's a lot of debate as to who the father of Romulus and Remus was. Some legends say that their father was the god Mars, who took Rhea Silvia by force. Some say that it was the half man-half god Hercules who fathered Rhea Silvia's sons.

Hercules

Some authors say that she was forced to be with an unknown man but then claimed that her sons were divinely conceived. In any case, Rhea Silvia became pregnant with Romulus and Remus.

WHAT HAPPENED TO RHEA SILVIA?

When a Vestal Virgin broke her vows of chastity for any reason, she was condemned to die a horrible death by being buried while she was still alive. However, Amulius who was now king, didn't want the god Mars or the demigod Hercules to be angry and come after him. So, instead, he threw Rhea Silvia in prison and ordered that her twins be put to death by being thrown into the river.

Romulus and Remus

He thought that if they died by nature instead of by the sword, the gods wouldn't punish him or the city of Alba Longa.

WHAT HAPPENED TO ROMULUS AND REMUS?

A servant was ordered to throw Romulus and Remus in the river. There are different versions of the legend here, but in every case, the servant takes pity on the two infant boys. The servant can't bear to kill them and instead puts them into a basket and places them into the Tiber River.

Tiber River

Palatine Hill

ROMULUS AND REMUS ARE DISCOVERED

The basket that was carrying the twins was swept along the waves of the river, but somehow Tibernus, the river god, calmed the waters and made sure they were safe. They landed in the roots of a fig tree at the base of the Palatine Hill.

There in the swamp, they were discovered by a female wolf that fed them her milk just as if they were her pups. They were also fed by a woodpecker that brought them figs off the tree. To this day, the image of Romulus and Remus being fed by the wolf is a famous image and represents Rome.

ROMULUS FREES REMUS FROM CAPTURE

A shepherd by the name of Faustulus and his wife Acca Larentia found the boys and took them in as adopted sons. They grew up to be shepherds too. One day as they were caring for the sheep, the king's shepherds started a fight with them and then captured Remus. Remus was brought before King Amulius.

Of course, the king didn't recognize that this young man was the son of Rhea Silvia. He had thought that the twins were drowned in the river many years before. In the meantime, Romulus had gathered up a force of local shepherds and went forth to free his brother and to kill the king.

ROMULUS AND REMUS ARGUE

The citizens of Alba Longa wanted the twins to reign as kings, but instead they restored King Numitor to his throne. They decided to begin their own city and went in search of a good location. Romulus wished to have the city's foundation be located at Palatine Hill.

Remus, however, wanted the city to built at Aventine Hill. To settle their disagreement, they decided to follow the practice of augury. Augury was the process of observing the flight path of birds to make predictions. When the observer or augur looked at the birds he was "taking the auspices" to determine whether it was a good or evil omen.

Aventine Hill

Each brother prepared a sacred spot on their respective hills to wait and observe passing birds. Remus first saw six birds and then Romulus saw twelve. However, the brothers still argued. Romulus thought that since he saw six more birds than his brother that the hill should be his choice, which was Palatine hill. Remus disagreed since he saw his birds first. He thought the choice should still be Aventine. They didn't settle the argument so Romulus started to dig trenches and construct walls around Palatine Hill.

THE DEATH OF REMUS

Unfortunately, Remus couldn't let the situation go. He started to make fun of the walls that Romulus was building. He would jump over them and make rude comments to his brother. At this point, there are various versions of the story. In one version, Remus dies after he falls from jumping up over the wall.

COGITA MORI

St. Jerome

This was thought to be a clear sign from the gods that the city of Rome was fated to be one of power. According to the writings of St. Jerome, Remus was killed by a spade thrown from one of his brother's supporters, either Celer or Fabius. Romulus is grief stricken now that is brother is dead. Many versions of the story say that Romulus kills his own brother. This event marks the founding of the city of Rome in the year 753 BC.

THE FOUNDING OF ROME

Romulus named the new city after himself. He created a government system that included senators as well as patricians who were high-class aristocrats. The city became very popular and the number of people living there grew rapidly.

La mu la

Tybens fluuius

S. al sus

Runaway slaves, criminals, and other exiles came to live there so the population was almost all male. It was a violent and rough city and women were not attracted to come there. However, the men wanted women for wives and to bear children for them. They came up with a daring plan to bring some women to the city.

THE SABINE WOMEN

The Romans invited the Sabians, a neighboring tribe, to a festival inside the walls of the city. As soon as they got inside, the Romans attacked the Sabian men and killed them.

They grabbed the women and took them away by force. The Sabian men who survived the attack returned to their city to get help, but this was Rome's first victorious battle.

However, this wasn't the end of the story. The Sabians devised a way to get back into the city. The Roman commander of the Capitoline citadel had a daughter. She promised to open the gates for the Sabians if they gave her any jewelry they wore on their left hands and arms. She expected to receive gold rings and bracelets, but instead she was crushed to death by the large shields of the Sabians as they marched through Rome's gates.

Pyramid of Caius Cestius in Rome

Rome almost fell to the Sabians led by their king, Titus Tatius. Romulus prayed to the great god Jupiter for help and the Romans were victorious. However, there was a problem. The Sabine women didn't want to go back to their tribe. They were helping their Roman husbands to win the battle!

So both sides formed a truce. Tatius and Romulus agreed to join forces and they both ruled together for five years. This was a time of peace in Rome and they shared gods, their use of the calendar, and even military strategies.

THE LEGACY OF ROMULUS AND REMUS

Today, we may never know which parts of this story are true and which parts are legend. What is true is that the story of Romulus and Remus was treated with admiration by the Ancient Romans and became the subject of famous works of literature and art.

Awesome! Now you know more about the founding of Rome by the twins Romulus and Remus. You can find more books about Ancient Rome from Baby Professor by searching the website of your favorite book retailer.

Visit

BABY PROFESSOR
EDUCATION KIDS

www.BabyProfessorBooks.com

to download Free Baby Professor eBooks
and view our catalog of new and exciting
Children's Books

Made in the USA
San Bernardino, CA
18 March 2019